# SEAHOUSES

# Seahouses

RICHARD BARNETT

*Valley Press*

First published in 2015 by Valley Press
Woodend, The Crescent, Scarborough, YO11 2PW
www.valleypressuk.com

First edition, first printing (February 2015)

ISBN 978-1-908853-46-2
Cat. no. VP0071

A CIP record for this book is available from the British Library.

Printed and bound in the EU by Pulsio, Paris.

www.valleypressuk.com/authors/richardbarnett

# Contents

# Acknowledgements

I'm grateful to the Poetry Society's SW13 Stanza and the Nevada Street Poets for their support. Through readings and discussions Liz Beardsworth, Caroline Essex, and John & Alex Broadbent all made 'Seahouses' measurably shorter and immeasurably better. These poems would not have been written without the friendship and encouragement of Michael Neve, Victoria Coombes, Thea Vidnes, and Theresia Hofer, given generously over more than a decade. 'Falling' is for Michael, 'Below The Falls' for Victoria, and 'Cloud Study, Hampstead Heath' for Thea and Resi. Kelley Swain has been magnificently infuriating and infuriatingly magnificent.

An earlier version of 'New River Songs' was published in the 2006 Templar Poetry competition anthology *Piqué*. 'Daybreak', 'Grace', and 'Pitcairn' were published in the 2007 Poetry Society SW13 Stanza anthology *Barnestorm*. 'Cloud Study, Hampstead Heath' and an earlier version of 'Not April, January' were published in *The London Magazine*, August / September 2009. A version of 'Lingo' was published in *3:AM Magazine* in November 2014. An earlier version of 'Seahouses' received the 2006 Promis Prize, and this collection was shortlisted for the 2013 Poetry Business book and pamphlet competition.

'Seahouses' takes lines or images from *The Tempest*, *King Lear*, Daniel Defoe's *The Storm*, JM Synge's *The Aran Islands*, William Hazlitt's essays, MR James' 'Oh Whistle and I'll Come to You, My Lad' and 'A Warning to the Curious', Anne Carson's *Plainwater*, and the traditional song 'Black is the Colour of My True Love's Hair'. 'You Do Not Do' takes its title from Sylvia Plath's 'Daddy'. 'A Line Made by Walking' takes its title from Richard Long's 1967 photograph. 'Borges' Tiger, Hockney's Leopard' refers to Jorge Luis Borges' 'Dreamtigers' and David Hockney's 'Picture Emphasising Stillness', and reworks a line attributed to St Augustine. The poems in 'Lingo' are made from example sentences in Noam Chomsky's *Topics in the Theory of Generative Grammar* and *Current Issues in Linguistic Theory*. 'Second Inaugural' and 'Falling' rework lines from documentary films by Jonathan Meades.

*for Kelley Swain*

# A Line Made By Walking

*after Richard Long*

Paths are ghosts. To walk
is to be haunted, to haunt.

>When you come, we go, leaving
>the presence of an absence. Our gift.

Sweet exhalation of moss and leafmould,
soft, secluding silence between steps.

>We find ourselves in untenanted mirrors,
>in the darkness between frames of a film.

Light dissolving behind,
shadows falling in front.

>The wind's plainsong in broken tracery,
>the breath of owls and mice in empty loom-sheds.

Leaves displaced, dust unsettled,
a whispering like chalk on slate.

>Our steps in yours, pulse-paced, hands
>always reaching out, just out of reach.

Would you rather be haunted or alone?
The oldest paths will take you home,

>if home is where you want to go.

# Falling

Unforecast snow beneath my shoe, beneath snow, ice,
beneath the ice a few skeletal leaves, and then
Euston Square – though today it might be anywhere.
Is this here all the time? This world uncovered by a covering,
this world of frost-slapped surfaces and faces,
of snow-embarrassed concrete, coy and soft?

No time to ask, of course. That came and passed at four,
when salt-trucks thawed the roadways of our dreams
and each street-lamp was a snow-globe, glowing sodium.
But dawn and dream broke one another, and ice,
like time, will have its way with each of us –

The thin grey workday line of coats and boots
are living, just for now, through limbs and soles,
devoting secret, strained attention to the world
of not-quite-right angles, subtly snarled,
and gravity, governess (who teaches us
the bruised amiability of the fallen), and –

A wild, abrupt, unconscious arabesque; call it falling,
the world inverted and in a moment grasped,
my fingers reaching out through air to trace
a strange new geometry, the heart of longing and belonging,
    like falling in love.

## Pitcairn

Take this, eat. It is not my body
but the breadfruit.
Soft, intoxicating, soporific –
our windfallen consolation.

Without the breadfruit tree,
we would have nothing –
no shade, no palisade,
no spears, no pyre,

and when we fight, we fight
because we do not share one belly.
But when we sleep, we slip
the moorings of our separateness –

becoming dreamtime breadfruit,
drum-tight bellies curled together,
each complicit, each soothed,
each a bud of the common vine.

And if you were to break the night's still waters,
to wake and pull yourself from clumps of vinous limbs,
if you walked, in your brass and worn blue broadcloth,
watching what you thought was Hesperus,

Vesper, the mourning star, rounding the ecliptic,
would you sit on the bare sand, thinking of breadfruit?

## Below the Falls

The river running all night, rising
all night, in spate, and the sound –
a steady sound, like a solid colour –
carried to my room, on the far side of the house.

Seven hours sleepless, I hear it still and fast,
this sound of sound, and see
the black hollow behind the falls,
the black bowl below the falls

where stones clash amongst roach and trout,
flecks of silver flashing in a whirl of slate –
the river's fugue, its variations on water.

## Daybreak

As the rain began to fall she woke,
feeling in her belly a kick (hunger?
resistance to new form?)
and on her lips an unfamiliar tang.

Our bodies are made of earth.
Our hair and bones remain and
everything else goes back to earth.
Not everything, she thought,
not yet.

He slept. She slipped out of bed,
for a moment thought of kicking him.
Behind the clouds the sky glowed
as in the hour before daybreak,
before light and shade.

## Love Without Mercy

Twelve years into his exile Morville's wife
discovers, in the rose-garden at dusk,
her husband kneeling, silent, bloodied, blind.
Tracing the line of what had been his sight
she lights upon the crag where, every day,
he saw in stone the Bishop's dying gaze.

After this, they say, he finds some peace,
but each night in his chamber, silk and straw,

he burns. Passing from sightless wakefulness
to dreams of fatal clarity, he moves
through silent, incensed cloisters to the place
where Becket kneels. And as he lifts his sword
the Bishop turns, and Morville is pierced through –
the gaze of those lion-eyes, that merciless love.

# Borges' Tiger, Hockney's Leopard

'Oh, incompetence! My dreams never seem to
engender the creature I so hunger for.'
– Jorge Luis Borges, 'Dreamtigers'


Aged eight, in fever, Borges dreamed a tiger
and the tiger stepped from the jungle of his dream
into his room. In the roaring of his blood
one tiger became a multitude, a chaos.
Tigers padded along his nerves,
purred in his ears, tumbled in his belly.

Hockney whispers *They are perfectly safe it is a still!*
as the painted leopard in its painted desert
springs for all time on two painted tramps
(who are either oblivious or assured
of immortality). Do not despair,
they mutter, do not presume.

## Cloud Study, Hampstead Heath

Today is made of light and air
and water underfoot. A mosaic
of leaves in furnace colours
marks the path up to the Heath.

He darts ahead, a solo skirmish-line
of clockwork ecstasy. Her steps are slower:
her soft brown shoes, rounded as rabbits,
nose for the safest holds.

From her bench the City opens like a pop-up book.
She watches him. He is a sycamore key,
dancing on air, so small, so slight,
that the wind must surely carry him away.

A rackety gust, the echo of a playground,
snatches his kite and tosses it over his head.
Lifted up to heaven, it drops a line to him,
and for a while,
                 as light and air remain,
he flies.

## Poem on Selling a Guitar

In the shop window, in someone else's eyes,
it will seem full of music. My fingertips
will forget the strings, but for a time
my shoulders will recall the heft.

What remains of a song,
when you find you cannot sing it?

## New River Songs

DEATH EXHAUSTED STOP HELL
FULL STOP HEAVEN NOT WHAT
IT WAS STOP TRY LONDON –

It is raining. It is always raining,
slick on the streets, sheets of rain over the City,
galaxies drifting in half-drunk pints.

A chessman with crazed ivory skin
bites his shield forever in the dark museum.


§


Quick and dark the river runs,
rain coming down and the window open –
another reason not to linger.

A black cat crouches like a scrawled signature.
Did we have to go looking
for dark energy?

She is pulling black tights
over her ankle forever.

Make a new river and
step into it – what's so hard
about that? What are you scared of?

If I cannot cry about it,
stepping into the rain, perhaps
it is not sad. Perhaps it is not.

An ice-cream van passes in the next street,
its chime the shade of summertime.


§


Looking down from a plane,
banking east over the estuary,
knowing she's down there –

as if the end, when it comes,
is not obliteration but a shattering,
pieces of us flung out through the world,

glimpsed in bus windows as they slide by.
What I don't see, I don't miss. I don't.

City of ghosts and restless water,
those gusts of bus-warm air,
the dead watching from the upper deck.

We are never still,
we do not dream,
we do not see the stars.

We see the empty floors of high-rise blocks
as the dusk comes on.


§


Autocorrect tries to help:

~~hunted~~ haunted
~~scared~~ sacred
~~untied~~ united

~~embarrassed~~ embraced
~~libelling~~ liebling
~~loser~~ lover

~~suckered~~ succoured
~~austerity~~ posterity

If you wanted to forget, would you be writing?
Forgive me this cheap conjuring trick,
pulling you out of my hat, my heart,

copying a copy of a copy.
A slender girl in a red raincoat, a stab of recognition,
leaf smoke curling into nothing,

a tea light burning in a window,
a slow unblinding. None of this will save us.


§


So let's pretend I'm holding out magnificently –
I will not come in off the swings,
I will sit on the swings in the rain

and recall the worn green paint
on the handles of the roundabout,
dumbly hot in August, crisply cold in March.

Turning these words like a conker in my hands,
that familiar childish shape, that gloss, that loss.

# Tomorrow

'The workers are destroying the machines!'
– Intertitle from *Metropolis* (1927)

tomorrow I will have unlimited data | tomorrow we will all go wildswimming | tomorrow we will vote in important elections | tomorrow we will print our own tickets to the festival | tomorrow we will keep bees for all the wrong reasons | tomorrow we will think and die in crowds | tomorrow we will smear our littleness across the stars | tomorrow we will gamify your breakdown

tomorrow is no laughing matter | tomorrow your fears will be exposed as inadequate | tomorrow will leave you more tradeable | tomorrow will be obscured by billboards | tomorrow does not need us but it does need me | tomorrow is subject to receipt of funding streams | tomorrow demands full compliance | tomorrow we will have rights

tomorrow there will be no more feast days | tomorrow we will not need to live for one another | tomorrow we will meet the stakeholders | tomorrow our smiles will be fixed | tomorrow we will have forgotten how it feels | tomorrow we will all be collaborators | tomorrow we will have stopped before it is too late | tomorrow I will have forgotten why I am so angry | tomorrow there will be no more words in private

## Second Inaugural

You know the disappointment of the Pacific. You crawl on
bright clear planes of colour. You are penitent in your
Klansman's hood. You have eaten everything, and had
your meal for free.

You have shot your youngest son in the head. You have his
blood on your gloves, and curds of his brain. You are all
murderers. Your children are all murderers, soldiers. In
the evening you sit and eat together.

You, Jack, are the man on the grassy knoll. You draw a bead
on the back of your handsome head. You plunge yourself
into history like the body of a jet plane. Still you are hung
up on grace.

# You Do Not Do

Things bend or else
they break
and you cannot bend.
Heroism, of a sort,
walking on
broken glass
and bellowing
for pity –

'Not this
old song again.'
Yes,
this old
corrosive
song –
the one
you taught me.

Afraid of crying,
you bit out
your tongue
and you are angry
because
I will not
bite out
my own?

I jump,
you push,
your will,
my inheritance.
I light a black candle
for you.
I wish you'd
succeeded.

# Nocturne

Show me the bodies of fast-food workers at night,
taut and sparse, dancing in fluorescent light.

Show me the supervisor, an older man,
south Indian maybe, streaks of grey in his beard –

His trousers cling to his buttocks like a Bernini marble.
His self-possession seems like heroism.

## January, Not April

has the cruellest mouth. Or mouths –
two-faced, both looking away

January sits in his overcoat
January sits in the waiting room
January has read all the magazines

January needs his tooth filled
January wants the needle in his gum

# Lingo

Three poems made from example sentences in Noam Chomsky's
*Topics in the Theory of Generative Grammar* and *Current Issues
in Linguistic Theory.*


1.


what disturbed John was being disregarded by everyone
everyone regards John as incompetent
everyone regards us as incompetent
the police were ordered to stop drinking after midnight

John didn't find the book
John was frightened by the new methods
John read the book and so did Bill
Bill was persuaded by John to leave

Bill was a farmer and so was John
John compelled
the shooting of the hunters
I expected it

the car was stolen by the boy
by the tallest of all the boys in the school
the car in the garage was kept by John
the garage that John kept the car in was demolished

the man who quit work was fired
someone find the man
who did he know who has something of yours?
John doesn't know how good meat tastes

2.

John is eating
his car was stolen

John is easy to please
John is eager to please

John pleases someone
this pleases John

John pleases everyone
John is easy (eager) for us to please

this knife is very difficult to cut (meat) with
they don't know how good meat tastes

3.

John admires someone
who admires who(m)?
which boys are in the room
you know the boy with (who has) a scar
I know a boy who was expelled
he found something of yours
what did he find of yours?
he found someone else
what else did he find?
he found someone of yours
who did he find of yours?
he found a boy
he found a friend of yours

his rejecting the offer surprised me
Mary saw the boy walking towards the railroad station
her car was stolen
what presumably did Bill see?
presumably Bill saw something
I don't approve of his drinking (cooking, driving etc)
his refusal to participate
his rejection of the offer
his destruction of property

the clever boy saw the friendly man

the book is what I want
I want the book

# Longshore Drift

He pulls his sleeves down over perished hands
(cuffs frayed, scuffed black, his elbows wearing through)
and trails along the dry-docked Sunday strand.
He summons whispers, echoes to pursue
down to the shore – another refugee?
But he finds only silence and the sea
where mocking waves break softly, two by two.

An hour – by foot, that is – along the cliffs
(stacked books, cracked pages crumbling, grey-faced)
she lingers, her eyes lost in longshore drift.
She conjures mares'-tails, mackerel, antique lace,
the froth on pints of bitter, wide bare sands.
She pulls her sleeves down over perished hands
and finds, for warmth, the ghost of an embrace.

## Grace

The absence of you
breaks the bread of my love.

The presence of you
consumes me.

## Seahouses

'The world is full of abandoned meanings.'
– Don Delillo, *White Noise*

Will you come with me? Everybody
Comes with me, eventually.

> A bare room, cracked white walls, rough brick floor,
> and in the centre of the floor an old brass bed. By the
> foot of the bed a pair of doors open on to a patch of
> grass, and beyond it a shore of sand. The sun has set,
> and lightning fires the clouds from within. Thunder
> is felt, not heard, and the faces of the figures on the
> bed are shadowed. The storm comes closer, and
> a thunderbolt strikes a tree along the shore. One
> wakes, slips out of bed, moves to the door.

The sea gets into everything. A wave breaks on the rocks
And wakes from a dream of drowning.
Voices on the wind, and red sails at the skyline:
Who is coming, who is this who is coming?

I, darkmouth, deepsalvaged, still
Some touch of nothingness about me

Here my fishbelly, caulked and clinkered,
And here my glorious sheer and rakish rig

My consort soul, composite,
Motion and rest incarved by craft

Will you come with me? Everybody
Comes with me, eventually

2.

> Boats are everywhere this morning. Cobles pulled up
> on the sand, their names painted on their gunwhales.
> Old cutters stand as sheds, crammed with bikes and
> the smell of rust and beeswax. Fibreglass tenders
> filled with dirt and daffodils. The fishwives sing
> as they wrap chips for boys out of school. I like
> listening to people when they don't know they're
> being heard, when they're singing for themselves.

These are, so I am told, the choices I have made
In some time and territory beyond my recollection.
A blanket, deckchair, unmade day: the cruel
Usual punishment for England's dreaming.
Run aground, weathering to sand, backed
Between stone quays, the arms
Of a weak, grey, unpropitiated god

    Perhaps, yes, perhaps | yes, yes, perhaps

Self-sufficient, distant sea,
Withdraw and overwhelm, itself it solves,
Wreck and return, and so two deaths.
She drifts, stranded and swamped, by night,
She sees him, lost, an empty chair across a table.
He drifts, chest-deep, salt ice, aged and ageless,
Dissolving back into the deepening swell

    Perhaps, yes, perhaps | yes, yes, perhaps

3.

> My first job, every year, when I get here, is to
> weatherproof the hull. This year was slow, wood and
> pitch weren't getting on. I kept finding myself with a
> rollup and a mug of tea, staring out at the gorse and
> marram running down to the beach. She's not a boat
> anymore, she's half a boat, and now she's my hut.
> There's an old hatch in the floor, the deck, I mean,
> where I can bury my feet in the shingle.

What do you see?

Peeling saltrusty white pain ragged flags children
concrete 10p telescopes paper windspinners relentless
heat like '76 parasols windbreaks bottleglass
carbuncles deckchair spinnakers bellying out swifts
seagulls sanderlings chattering blackbird bursting from
gorse yellow flowers yellow beak yellow –

Or tall windows, tall masts framed in windows,
The inconstant moon and the obsolete stars –
Remembered absences, as gulls,
Once the ghosts of sailors, now just gulls,
Hang in the air.

And through this commerce we become
Both those who sail and those who wait –
Some still, some calling, drawing back,
Broken-backed boats on a sandy bay.

4.

Late on a winter day we crossed the causeway
And, reaching the dunes, turned to watch the tide
Paw at our footprints –

Where the slow sand sea breaks on the beach
A lifebelt on its gibbet frames a pilgrim's cross
Against the night –

The waves that break and flow like hair
Over the sand and the black rocks
Sing across the shore –

The sea that sings across this shore
Is the sea that old men, shawled in Fair Isle blankets,
Gaze on from their deckchairs –

The broken mirror of the world

It wouldn't be so bad if your eyes could get used to it,
but every twenty minutes a bike with full headlights
will scream along the coast road, and everything
turns purple and white again. You can see the light
from televisions in windows, and then someone
gets up and pulls the blinds down. There's the sea, of
course, but there's also this pinking sound. At first
everyone always thinks it must be birds, but it's not
birds, it's the shrouds knocking against the metal
masts of yachts in the car park.

5.

A red sail and a dragon head
Prowling at the sealine:
Cuthbert kneels, closes his eyes, prays

That his soul might be made transparent,
That he might discern the muscled parts,
The wellmade parts, and that which has decayed

(And say he did call water from dry rock,
And say his corpse, eleven years in sand, was quick and
   supple –)

We all know what's down there, the ocean's
archive, and it comes up on the nets and on the
anchor shanks. The bed up here is different to
Dunstanburgh, and Dunstanburgh will be different
to Craster, and so on all the way around to here
again. When the land is soft it washes away like
nothing, but the rock lasts a little longer. I wonder
sometimes what it would be like if the water drew
back, even for half a minute.

*John Staveacre, James Morton, five heathen Danes, and some*
*Who from their dress and coin we took for Irish fishmen*
*Were buried here where they were found this day*

In the lee of the dunes
Some bones, some hair and broadcloth
Emerge, lie beneath the sun,
And sink back into the sand

6.

It's strange taking trippers out to the Farnes. A
fisherman never goes out with a full hold, so she's
different, she's slower, she wallows more and makes
them sick. It's alright, I tell them, everyone gets
sick on their first trip. I wasn't.

Singing through the stillness, through the warmth of dusk,
They came from the saltbeaten oak of the chapel door.
Lanterns along the cliffpath, strung across the headland,
Out to the lighthouse. Songs and words for crossing water,
To Christopher and now to Mary, star of the sea,
Our lady. Why do they offer themselves to the tides,
These fishers of men in their unrighted naves?

You hang on as long as you can

So as to keep faith with doubt. You grasp at anything,
At the restlessness of water's forms –
There is no end to remembrance, no end
To loss and its remembrance.
Beards jewelled with seaspray,
Hooks and eyes in the dark glistening deep,
And a whispering, now, in the chapel on the cliffs –

Trespass against us, against
Us, trespass against us

7.

Clouds far off, and more a dream
Than an assurance. I am standing water.
Teach me to flow. Sometimes I'll divide
And burn in many places. This fretful wind, now,
A fret of wind, murmurous waters,
Crossplay of breakers, cloud shadows on
The long, slow, gathering swell.

Though the seas threaten, they are
                                merciful.
Make not too rash a trial of me, for
            I am gentle and
not fearful.
            We had been safe, and for so long
Had seen        all things
                        quiet about us,
So, near the Goodwin, tired with the service of the night,
We slipt our sheet and fled the Downs.

Soon sail we had                        none, nor mast
                    withstanding:
        Our mate had
                    set up a jury    mizzen, but
            No canvas could bear        the fury of the wind.
Reel to and fro,
        stagger like a drunken man,
    Remembrance grievous, the burden intolerable,
Each one        drowned while he laboured,
Great ships aground,
        rent in pieces,
        the wrack of all.

Waters like

                    whole rivers      flood the air –

Bosun,

       bosun,      the spars

         Are fallen in on me –  a little more   in death

       Each seventh wave.

              My darling skinny      one,

You have    come when         I had you

       Least in mind.

Will you come with me?

            Forgive me,

Though I would do it all again, forgive me.

8.

> You just have to ride it. I only went overboard
> once, years ago, when I was a fisherman. Typical
> fisherman, I wasn't wearing a lifejacket, and we were
> miles from home off Terschelling. She rolled and I
> went in backwards over the side.

I drink the air before me, now the water,
Desperate for any deliverance. We do be afraid
Of the sea, and we do be drownded only now and again,
And we go out. Doing was my undoing, and now
We rise, my love, we rise again to air

   Between us nothing more or less than skin –
   Impossible to say where you end, where I begin

With new love comes imperfect intimacies,
The flowing, not the fixed, as flame bends to flame,
And will you not rise again, my love, are
You falling or am I? When will you
Give me up?

   Your falling is forgivable, forgiven –
   Impossible to say where you end, where I begin

No airy heaven, no ashen hell,
Which of us the ghost? I cannot tell,
Only a new voice calling out,
Calling 'As fresh meat loves salt,
I love you', my ship that ne'er returned –

I will go with you.

9.

> I was only in the water for a quarter hour but I was
> terrified. Seeing this huge boat, a forty-eight-foot
> cutter, pulling away from you when she's the only
> light. When they picked me up I sat for an hour
> trying to pull myself together. I knew I had to go
> back out, so I had to pull myself together.

Not remembering how I cried out
I will cry again. An empty chair,
once more, across a table, and I dissolve

*Black is the colour of my true love's hair*

He is the air and I am the feathers

*His face so soft and wondrous fair*

He is the water and I the waves

*The sweetest eyes and the gentlest hands*

He is the bed and I am the lovers

*I love the ground whereon he stands*

He is the earth and I the graves

I remember three years ago – I'm on the lifeboat
– we went out to a Norwegian lobster boat. No sign
of the crew. We pulled up all the pots, forty of them,
in case they'd been caught in the ropes and pulled
down, but nothing. I was sailing his boat back to the
harbour and his cup of coffee was on the dashboard,
half full and still steaming.

Will you come with me? Everybody
Comes with me, eventually.